Amazing
Questions & Answers

Science

Om
KIDZ

An imprint of Om Books International

Om KIDZ | Om **Books International**

Reprinted in 2024

Corporate & Editorial Office
A-12, Sector 64, Noida 201 301
Uttar Pradesh, India
Phone: +91 120 477 4100
Email: editorial@ombooks.com
Website: www.ombooksinternational.com

Sales Office
107, Ansari Road, Darya Ganj
New Delhi 110 002, India
Phone: +91 11 4000 9000
Email: sales@ombooks.com
Website: www.ombooks.com

© Om Books International 2019

ISBN: 978-93-52763-06-1

Printed in India

20 19 18 17 16 15 14 13 12 11 10

How?

How are candies made?

What?

Why are tyres black?

What is air made of?

Why?

When?

When do objects rust?

CONTENTS

How do helium balloons rise so high?

Because helium is lighter than air! Some balloons are not filled with air but a gas called helium. A balloon filled with helium weighs less than the same sized balloon filled with air. This makes the helium balloon float upwards and rise high.

Find out

Is there any gas other than helium that is lighter than air?

Pocket fact

Around the world!
In 1986, a plane called Voyager flew all around the world without having to land or refuel even once!

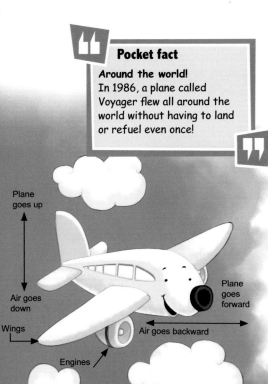

Plane goes up

Air goes down

Wings

Engines

Plane goes forward

Air goes backward

How does a plane take off and fly?

With the help of its engine and wings! The engines of a plane are designed in such a way that they help it move forward at high speed. They produce a force called thrust which gives the plane horizontal movement. When the plane starts moving, the air flows rapidly over its wings. This throws the air towards the ground, generating an upward force called lift. The plane takes off and the lift overcomes the plane's weight, holding it in the sky.

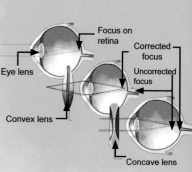

Focus on retina

Corrected focus

Uncorrected focus

Eye lens

Convex lens

Concave lens

How do contact lenses work?

By changing the direction of light rays and focusing them on the retina! Contact lenses are thin discs made of plastic. Unlike spectacles, they sit directly on the cornea of your eye and help correct eyesight problems by diverging or converging light rays. This helps the eye focus light directly on the retina where the image is formed which helps you see clearly.

Pocket fact

Who made it?
In the year 1887, German physiologist Adolf Fick invented contact lenses. They were made of glass and were called scleral lens. They were named so because they covered the sclera, the white part of the eye.

Try this

Take two mirrors and a candle. Place one mirror in front and the other behind the candle. How many candles do you see in the mirrors now?

How does my reflection look inverted in a spoon?

That's because the spoon is not straight! Spoons are curved in such a way that they bend inward. The bowl-shape is incapable of reflecting your image straight, like a mirror does. When you see yourself in a spoon, the bottom of the spoon is pointed towards your forehead and the top of the spoon is pointed towards your chin. Your chin is reflected at the bottom and your forehead at the top making your reflection inverted!

True North

Magnetic North

Magnetic South

True South

Find out

How was the compass useful to sailors in ancient times?

Its needle does the trick! Magnets are attracted toward other magnets and the needle of a compass is a magnet too. Our planet Earth is a huge magnet that attracts the needle. Earth has two poles: north and south, both of which are magnetic. The North Pole of the Earth attracts the compass needle towards it. This is why the compass always points north!

Pocket fact

In 1714, German physicist Daniel Gabriel Fahrenheit, invented the mercury thermometer. The temperature scale—Fahrenheit—bears his name!

How does a thermometer detect fever?

It measures the rise in temperature! Your normal body temperature is 98.4 °Fahrenheit. When you have fever, your body temperature rises above normal and the thermometer detects this rise. It has liquid mercury in a long clear tube. The mercury expands and rises up when it comes in contact with heat. So, when the thermometer is put in your mouth, mercury in the tube rises if you have fever. The scale on the thermometer tells us what the temperature is.

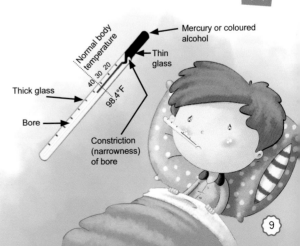

Normal body temperature

Mercury or coloured alcohol

Thin glass

Thick glass

Bore

98.4°F

Constriction (narrowness) of bore

How are candies made?

The yummy candies you enjoy are mostly made of sugar! Sugar is boiled to a really high temperature and when it becomes very hot, fruit flavours, food colours and sometimes even nuts are added. The boiling hot sugar is then poured into moulds to give it shape. It is then wrapped in colourful paper and ready to be eaten. Yuummm!

Find out

When was toothpaste invented?

Pocket fact

The largest toffee!
On 17 September 2002, Susie's South Forty Confections, USA, created the largest piece of candy. It weighed around 1,330 kilograms!

How does toothpaste fight germs?

In three easy steps! The first step is to scrub away the grime. Toothpaste contains abrasives that scrub away the dirt and remove stains from your teeth. The second is the action of fluoride. Toothpaste contains fluoride which protects the tooth enamel by forming a layer over it to protect it from germ attack. It also freshens your breath and gives you the perfect smile!

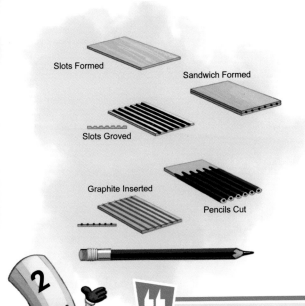

Slots Formed

Sandwich Formed

Slots Groved

Graphite Inserted

Pencils Cut

How was the first pencil made?

By placing graphite into wooden holders! The first pencil was invented in 1564 in England. A huge graphite mine was discovered in Borrowdale, Cumbria, England. The graphite was first mined and sawn into sheets, then cut into square rods. These rods were inserted into hand-carved wooden holders, giving birth to the new writing tool, pencil!

Pocket fact

A pencil with gold and diamonds!
A limited edition pencil, the 'Perfect Pencil' by the company Faber-Castell is world's most expensive pencil, made with white gold and diamonds.

How does a pencil eraser work?

By scratching! Pencil easers are mostly made of rubber, plastic or vinyl. Some erasers have abrasive substances in them. When you rub an eraser over something you have written, the abrasive scratches it away. On the other hand, some erasers are sticky. The dark lines of pencil graphite stick to these erasers and are picked up when you rub them, making your writing disappear!

Find out

What does the number on the pencil indicate?

How do flexible fasteners work?

The small hooks and loops on its surface make it work! A flexible fasteners has two pieces—one with numerous small hooks made of flexible plastic and the other with loops that are made of soft fabric strings. When the two meet, the hooks and loops get tangled and stick to each other! This mechanism works because the hooks and loops are large in number. A single hook and loop can't give the same result.

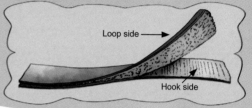

Loop side →

Hook side

Find out

Have you heard of electric blankets? What are they?

Pocket fact

Velcro is extensively used in army tanks. They are used to hold flashlights to the walls!

How do blankets keep me warm?

By slowing the heat transfer from your body! Your body constantly loses heat to the environment. A blanket prevents your body heat from being lost to your surroundings. At the same time, cold air from outside tries to carry your body heat away, but the blanket forms a barrier between you and the cold air and prevents this from happening. Till you're covered up well, your body heat keeps you warm, even if it's snowing outside!

Air

Blanket

Keeps warmth in

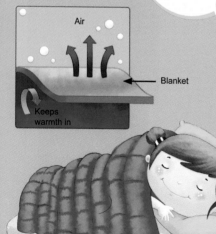

How does a zipper work?

With the help of its teeth! Every zipper has two parts: slide—the part that you pull and teeth—on either side of the item being zipped. The teeth of a zipper are shaped like little hooks! They're made such, so they can hook and unhook from each other as you slide it up and down! When you pull the zipper up, it brings the two rows of teeth together and the zip gets closed. When you pull the zipper down, it pulls the teeth away to unzip!

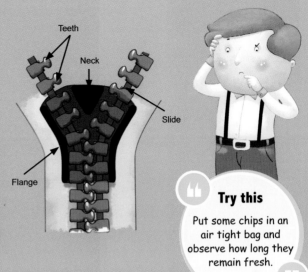

Teeth

Neck

Slide

Flange

Try this

Put some chips in an air tight bag and observe how long they remain fresh.

Pocket fact

Elias Howe was the inventor of zipper and sewing machine. He made an earlier form of the zipper, called The Automatic, Continuous Clothing Closure in 1851. He was so occupied in working on his sewing machine that he abandoned the zipper.

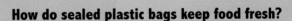

How do sealed plastic bags keep food fresh?

By keeping the air out! Some plastic bags have a sealing mechanism like a plastic zipper that lets you seal it. This keeps the air out. Food stays fresh for long when it is kept away from air. Bacteria and other microbes in the air, break down food items when they come in contact with them. Sealed plastic bags keep air and its organisms from getting to your food and keep them fresh!

Find out

Who invented the ceiling fan?

Off

On   On

Terminal A   Terminal B

Common Terminal

How does a switch work?

By acting like a gate to control the flow of electricity! You need electricity to make an electric appliance work. Electricity flows through circuits that are like pathways made of wires and a switch. The switch is used to open and close this circuit. When you turn on a switch, it closes the circuit connected to the appliance and current flows through it, thus making it work.

Pocket fact

If a lamp on the Moon (384,400 kilometres away) is connected to a switch on Earth, it would take only 1.28 seconds for it to light up! This is because electricity travels at an incredible speed of 299,338 kilometres per second.

How does a fan work to cool me off?

By creating a cooling effect! The fan does not cool the room at all but just creates a cooling effect! When it's hot, your body loses heat in the form of sweat. When you switch on a fan, its circular motion blows the air all around the room. This makes it easier for sweat to evaporate from your skin and you feel cool. The more the evaporation, the cooler you feel!

How does a car horn honk?

An electromagnet makes it honk! The horn of a car is usually electric and controlled by a flat circular steel diaphragm. The diaphragm has an electromagnet acting upon it and is attached to a contactor that repeatedly stops flow of current to the electromagnet. When you press the horn, the electromagnet causes the diaphragm to move towards it and oscillate back and forth, producing the honking sound.

HONK!

HONK!

Diaphragm

Armature

Switch

Contact

Find out

Which is the fastest car in the world?

Pocket fact

In 1886, Carl Benz made the first modern car called the Benz Patent-Motorwagen.
It is said that in 1888 Carl Benz's wife took this car for a test drive, made minor repairs along the way and gave him some suggestions to improve it.

How does a car move?

A car engine has cylinders on a crankshaft. When the engine runs, the pistons of the car compress gas and air in the cylinder. Then, the spark plug ignites the compressed gas mixture, and a small explosion occurs that pushes the piston in the opposite direction. This turns the crankshaft, which turns a fly wheel. Now, the energy produced in this explosion is transferred to the wheels of the car and vroooom it goes!

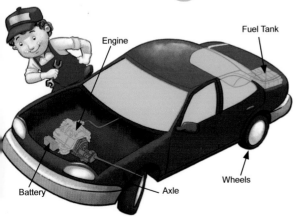

Engine

Fuel Tank

Wheels

Battery

Axle

How does a matchstick burn?

A matchstick has a small wooden stick body with a head made of sulfur, red phosphorus and glass powder. When it is struck against a rough surface, the glass powder produces heat. This converts a small amount of red phosphorus to white phosphorus, which quickly catches fire and releases oxygen. Then, the sulfur in the head catches fire and makes the matchstick burn!

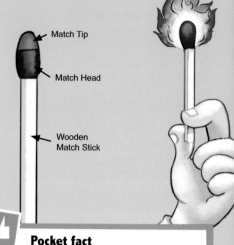

Match Tip

Match Head

Wooden Match Stick

Find out

What do the Dutch call a matchstick?

Pocket fact

The Sun provides more energy to Earth in an hour than all the energy used by people all over the world. The world only uses 17 terawatts of energy in a year whereas 120,000 terawatts reach the Earth's surface each day.

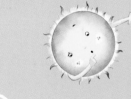

How do solar lights work?

Solar lights have solar cells that convert sunlight into direct electrical current! Solar cells can be seen as a dark panel on the top of a solar light. There are multiple layers of crystalline silicon and chemicals in a solar cell that create layers of negatively charged electrons and positively charged spaces. When sunlight passes through the solar cell, the positively charged spaces convert sunlight into electricity and make bulbs glow.

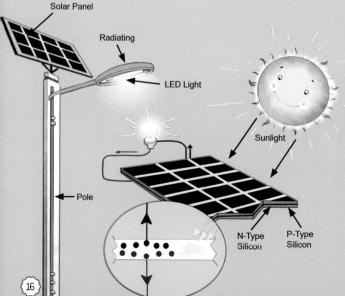

Solar Panel

Radiating

LED Light

Pole

Sunlight

N-Type Silicon

P-Type Silicon

How can a room become soundproof?

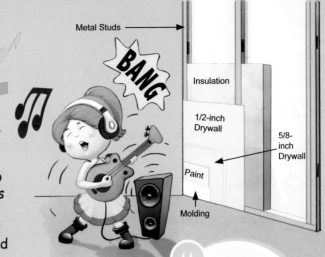

Metal Studs

Insulation

1/2-inch Drywall

5/8-inch Drywall

Paint

Molding

To make a room soundproof, soundboard laminate is applied to existing walls of the room. Thereafter, a two inch metal frame partition is constructed half inch away from the wall. Then, regular fibreglass insulation is placed between the wall and the partition and is sealed with a 5/8 inch drywall. This makes rooms soundproof.

Find out

Which of the following should be soundproof?
A supermarket
A music recording studio
A football stadium

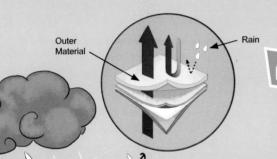

Outer Material

Rain

Pocket fact

Charles Macintosh is credited with inventing raincoats in 1823. The famous Macintosh raincoat was named after him.

How is a raincoat waterproof?

Raincoats are made of polyester, nylon, or rayon, specially treated to keep liquids away. The fabric is passed through rollers and dipped into chemicals. The chemical soaked fabric is then heated. Thereafter, it is again passed through rollers and cooled down. This makes the waterproofing chemicals permanently stick to the fabric and it is then turned into a raincoat for you!

How does a water fountain work?

A fountain sprays the water into the air or sometimes creates a waterfall effect. An outdoor fountain has a reservoir, a pump and a spinning impeller. When the fountain is started, the pump supplies power to draw water from the reservoir. The spinning impellor in the pump draws water in and spins it at a high speed. The water is forced out of the pump to the fountainhead and is sprayed into the air through a fine nozzle. It can also flow down as a waterfall in some fountains.

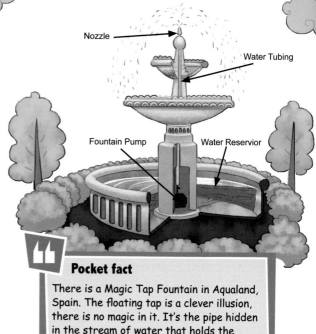

Nozzle

Water Tubing

Fountain Pump

Water Reservior

Pocket fact

There is a Magic Tap Fountain in Aqualand, Spain. The floating tap is a clever illusion, there is no magic in it. It's the pipe hidden in the stream of water that holds the fountain!

Find out

Why do taps leak sometimes?

Handle

Screw

Shaft

Seat

Thread

Washer Plate

Washer

Nut

How does the water stop when you close the tap?

The washer doesn't let it out! A tap has a screw on the top and a washer at the bottom. When you turn the tap on, the screw rises. This lifts the washer with it and lets the water gush up from the pipe and come out through the spout. When you turn the tap off, the screw pushes the washer back down onto the pipe and stops the flow of water.

How does a roller coaster work without an engine?

Two types of energies make it work! Before a rollercoaster ride begins, an electric winch winds the car to the top of the hill. The winch uses potential energy to hold the roller coaster on the hill. Once you are onboard, the cars are released and start to roll down. The weight of the car itself and Earth's gravity propels the car downwards. The energy that keeps the fun ride going is called kinetic energy!

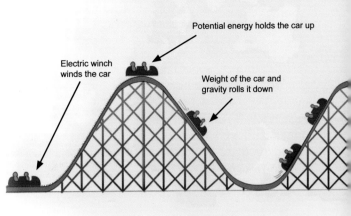

Potential energy holds the car up

Electric winch winds the car

Weight of the car and gravity rolls it down

Pocket fact

The biggest fall!
Kingda Ka roller coaster at Six Flags Great Adventure in Jackson, New Jersey, USA has a drop of 418 feet, highest amongst all roller coasters!

Find out

Why do bicycle wheels have spikes?

Rear brakes

Front brakes

How does my bicycle stop when I apply the brake?

You need to simply press the brake levers on the handlebars to stop your bicycle! Thin metal cables run to the back and front wheels and pull on small calipers in your bicycle. This forces thick rubber blocks to press against the wheels. Then, heat is generated between the blocks and the metal wheel rims due to friction. This brings your bicycle to a safe halt!

What makes cola fizzy?

It's the carbon dioxide! Cola has carbon dioxide gas dissolved in it. When the bottle is closed, the cola is under pressure, and so carbon dioxide does not escape the bottle. But when you open the bottle, it releases the pressure and carbon dioxide begins to escape in the form of rising bubbles. This is what makes cola fizzy. So, if you want your cola to fizz, keep the bottle shut!

Pocket fact

The first flavoured soft drink was made in the United States in 1807 by Townsend Speakman. The popular ingredients in the drink were birch bark, dandelions, ginger, lemon, coca and kola!

Try this

- Collect two pipe cleaners and soap water.
- Bend a pipe cleaner into a square and wrap the ends to hold it together.
- Now fold the other pipe cleaner in half and loop it around one side of the square.
- Twist the ends together to make a handle and use it as a bubble blower.
- Dip the bubble blower into the soap water and slowly blow through it.

What are soap bubbles made of?

Air wrapped in a soap film! A bubble is a pocket of soap and water filled with air. When soap and water mix together and air blows into it, a thin skin traps the air. This is what makes a bubble. A bubble has soap molecules all over its surface. A thin layer of water lies between the two layers of soap molecules. They work together to hold the air inside the bubble and make them float.

What makes fireworks colourful?

Chemicals! All fireworks are made of different chemicals. These chemicals glow in different colours when they are hot. Fireworks that contain the chemical sodium glow with yellow and orange colours. Those with potassium give out a purple glow, and those with iron, magnesium and aluminium glow in white and golden colours.

Find out

Why do fireworks make sound when they burn?

Pocket fact

Have you ever wondered what a flame would look like without gravity? Will it point upwards? The answer is no! The flame would appear round and blue in absence of gravity.

Cooler gases sink

Hot gases rise

Gravity

Gravity

What makes flames point upwards?

Its low density! Flames are hot gases that emit light. As a flame burns, it heats the surrounding gases. The hot air around the flame pushes up as it is less dense. Cool air is pulled down by gravity and gets closer to the flame and replaces the lighter gases that are pushed up. This makes the flame point upwards.

What is air made of?

Air is made up of different gases. Nitrogen accounts for 78% of the air, 21% of it is oxygen, essential for our survival. So what makes up the other 1%? Besides oxygen and nitrogen, air also has small amounts of other gases, like carbon dioxide, neon, helium and methane. You'll also find water vapour, pollen, dust and even microbes in it!

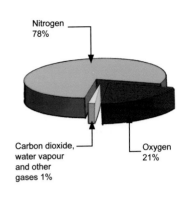

Nitrogen 78%

Carbon dioxide, water vapour and other gases 1%

Oxygen 21%

Action: Air rushes down

Reaction: Balloon goes up

Find out

Air has oxygen that is essential for breathing. What is the use of nitrogen?

What happens when I blow up a balloon and let it go?

When you blow a balloon, air occupies the space inside it and the balloon expands in size. The air then pushes against the inner surface of the balloon, building a pressure. The outside pressure balances the pressure inside. But when you let it go, the balloon quickly releases air and moves in the opposite direction.

Pocket fact

Swedish pharmacist Carl Wilhelm Scheele, British clergyman Joseph Priestley and French chemist Antoine Laurent Lavoisier, researched and discovered oxygen between 1770 and 1780. The name 'oxygen' was first used by Lavoisier in 1777.

What causes me to slip when I step on ice?

Lack of friction

Ice

The lack of friction! Friction is a force that occurs when two rough surfaces rub together. When the surfaces come in contact, they press up against each other and cause friction that helps you walk. But sometimes, a surface like ice may be smooth and lacks the roughness that you need to stay upright, this makes it very slippery to walk on.

Find out

We get natural adhesive from some trees. Can you name two such trees?

Pocket fact

Get, set, go!
When vehicles move, the air around them generates friction called air resistance that slows them down. Fast moving vehicles, such as cars, trains and airplanes are all designed with curved and sloping surfaces so that they can reduce the drag. This helps them to move faster and consume less fuel.

What makes glue stick things?

Glue is made from a fluid that changes to a solid state when it is dry. Most of the things that can be glued together have tiny ridges and bumps on their surface. When you apply glue to such a surface, it fills in all the ridges and bumps. Once the glue dries, it works like a strong bond grabbing hold of the two surfaces to keep it together.

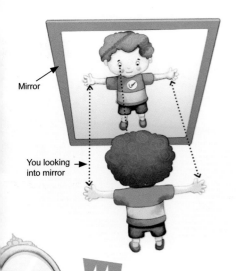

Mirror

You looking into mirror

What makes my right hand look like it is the left one in the mirror?

A mirror reflects exactly what is in front of it. When you stand in front of a mirror, light rays reflected by your left hand fall on the mirror and make a reflection straight at the spot where it falls. Similarly, rays from your right hand also follow the same reflection method. So, your right becomes left and left becomes right in the mirror. It is just the same as your friend standing opposite you holding your hands.

Pocket fact

Silvered-glass mirrors were first invented by a German chemist Justus von Liebig in 1835. He created an extremely thin layer of silver on glass using a chemical reaction. This made mirrors easily available for common people for the first time.

Try this

What would these letters look like when you see them in a mirror? The first one has been done for you.

F Ⅎ J
B _ A _

What makes me see through a glass door but not a wall?

Light! Light travels in a straight line and is reflected and absorbed by different objects. Since a glass door is transparent, light easily passes through it and we can see what is on the other side. When light falls on a wall, it is absorbed by the wall and cannot pass through it. So, we are unable to see what is on the other side of the wall.

What makes the popcorn 'pop'?

A tiny drop of water! Popcorn is not ordinary corn. It is the only type of corn that pops. Each grain of popcorn has a tiny droplet of water inside it, surrounded by a hard cover called hull. As you heat the popcorn, the water turns into steam. Since the steam can't escape the hard cover, the grain of corn pops.

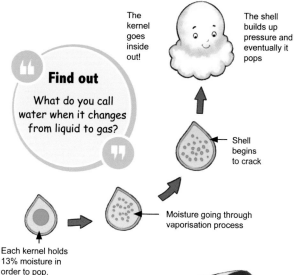

The kernel goes inside out!

The shell builds up pressure and eventually it pops

Find out

What do you call water when it changes from liquid to gas?

Shell begins to crack

Moisture going through vaporisation process

Each kernel holds 13% moisture in order to pop.

Pocket fact

Popcorn becomes mobile!
An inventor named Charles Cretors introduced the first moveable popcorn machine in 1893. The machine was introduced at the World's Columbian Exposition in Chicago.

What makes water droplets dance on a hot pan?

The droplets dance because they vaporise immediately on contact with the hot plate! When you sprinkle water on a hot pan, it forms an invisible layer that prevents it from boiling quickly. Due to this, drops of water hover over the surface of the pan. This makes the drops skid around the pan and it seems to dance!

What keeps me from floating in air?

Gravity pulls you down! Gravity is an invisible force that attracts any two objects found in the universe. The heavier the object, the stronger is its gravitational pull. Our planet, Earth, is very heavy and so it has a very strong gravitational pull. This makes everything on Earth stay in place and keeps you from floating in air.

Gravity

Gravity

Pocket fact

Lowest gravity on Earth! Parts of Hudson Bay and the surrounding regions of Quebec are areas with very low gravity on Earth.

Try this

Collect any 10 items, five of which you think will float on water and five that will sink. Take a bucket full of water and drop each of the 10 items one-by-one. Was your guess correct?

What makes a ship float on water?

Water's high density! Ships can float because they are less dense than water. When a ship is on water, two forces act upon it: a downward force of the ship and an upward force that's determined by the weight of the water displaced by the ship. When this upward force is more than the weight of the ship, it makes the ship float!

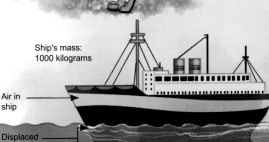

Ship's mass: 1000 kilograms

Air in ship

Displaced water

What turns milk sour?

An acid! Milk contains a type of sugar called lactose. When milk is boiled and stored in a cool place, lactobacillus, the bacteria present in milk, are killed and milk does not turn sour. But when milk is not boiled or left in a humid place, the bacteria grows easily, causing lactose to react with oxygen. This makes lactic acid. It is this lactic acid that turns milk sour.

Find out

Why do fruits rot?

Lactobacillus produces lactic acid

Pocket fact

Helpful bacteria!
Lactobacillus bacteria are not always harmful. This bacteria at the right temperature can change milk to curd!

What makes apples turn brown when cut?

A reaction with air! Apples and some other fruits contain an enzyme called tyrosinase. When apples are cut, this enzyme reacts with oxygen in the air and the iron-rich chemicals present in the apple. This reaction forms a brown coating on the surface of the apples.

What changes water into ice?

Loss of heat at 0 °Celsius!
Water is made of tiny particles
called molecules. When water
gets colder than 0 °Celsius, the
molecules of water lose their
energy. This brings them closer
together and makes them
move slow. They then form
a hexagonal pattern turning
water into ice.

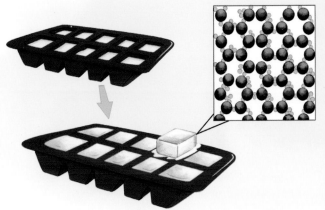

Pocket fact

Have you heard of anything
that can change air into
water? There's a billboard in
Peru that creates drinkable
water out of thin air!

Find out

What is water
made of?

What helps me pull out water with a straw?

It's the air pressure! When you
drink water using a straw, you
create a vacuum by sucking the
air out of it. Since there is air
outside, it creates pressure
around the straw. The outside
pressure of the straw is greater
than the pressure inside. This
pressure causes water to rise up
in the straw and gets pulled into
your mouth.

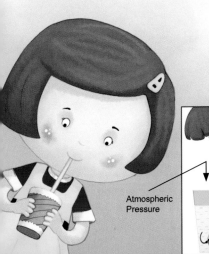

Atmospheric
Pressure

What gives rainbow its seven colours?

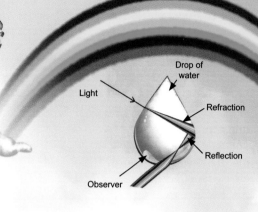

Light

Drop of water

Refraction

Reflection

Observer

Splitting of the sunlight! Sunlight is made of different colours but we cannot see them easily. When we pass sunlight through a prism or glass, it splits into a band of seven colours called spectrum. When it rains, raindrops act as tiny prisms. When sunlight passes through them, it breaks up into its spectrum and we see all the colours in the form of a rainbow.

The scattering of blue light by gas molecules in the atmosphere

Sunlight made of all colours

Find out

Why does the sky appear black at night even when there is moon to give light?

Pocket fact

Moonbows!
Moonbows are like rainbows which occur when the moon's light reflects through raindrops. This type of rainbow is rare because the moon's light usually isn't bright enough for a rainbow to form.

What makes the sky look blue?

It's the Sun! Blue colour in the sunlight spectrum travels in the form of short and small waves. When sunlight reaches the Earth's atmosphere, it gets scattered in all directions by the gases and particles in the Earth's air. This is what gives sky its blue colour in the day.

What makes an egg hard inside when it is boiled?

Eggs are made of proteins. When you boil an egg, the protein molecules get heated up and gain energy. It then forms strong bonds with all the other protein molecules around it. This is what we see as a hard, boiled egg!

Find out

What is an egg shell made of?

Pocket fact

Ping pong balls bounce higher than other balls. Table tennis players started using ping pong balls made of cellulose after James Gibb discovered the celluloid ball during a trip to the United States in 1901.

What makes a ball bounce?

Gravity and energy! Gravity pulls everything down towards the Earth. But when the ball falls down, it picks up energy before it reaches the ground and this energy needs to be used. So, when the ball touches the ground, the energy inside the ball pushes it and the ball bounces.

What is an easy way to lift heavy objects?

Pulleys! Sometimes it's not easy to lift heavy objects. This problem can be fixed with the help of a simple machine, like a pulley. A pulley consists of a wheel on a fixed axle, with a groove along the edges to guide a rope. It helps you lift heavy objects easily. When you put two or more wheels together, and run a rope around them, a great lifting machine is created!

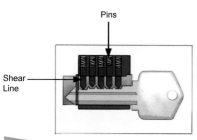

Find out

Are there any locks that can be opened without a key?

Pocket fact

We all take the credit!
Many people are credited with inventions of different locks. Just have a look.
Robert Barron in 1778: double-acting tumbler lock
Joseph Bramah in 1784: Bramah lock, unpickable for 67 years
Jeremiah Chubb in 1818: detector lock with high internal security
Linus Yale, Sr. in 1848: first pin tumbler lock
James Sargent in 1857 and 1873: first combination lock and first time lock mechanism
Samuel Segal in 1916: first jemmy-proof lock
Harry Soref in 1924: first padlock

What magic makes a key open a lock?

It's the teeth on the keys! Every key has a unique pattern of cuts or teeth that make it open the lock it belongs to. A lock has a track called shear line inside it. This shear line has spring-loaded pins that move up and down. The pattern on every key matches up to the pins on the inside of its lock. When the teeth fit into the shear line, the lock opens! When the teeth don't match up with the pins, the lock doesn't turn and a different key is needed!

What is the secret of shadows?

It's light blocked by objects! Light travels in a straight line and cannot pass through opaque objects. Since light cannot pass through the object, it creates a dark patch around it. This area where the light cannot reach is called a shadow.

Rays of light

Shadow

Pocket fact

Ben Franklin in 1752 developed a theory that lightning in the sky was the same static electricity that is generated by rubbing a comb on dry hair. He performed a kite experiment to test this which later came to be known as Franklin's famous kite experiment.

Try this

Set up a lamp and stand in front of it so you can cast a shadow on the wall behind you. Watch your shadow carefully. What happens when you move closer to the lamp or move away from it?

What makes bits of paper stick to a plastic comb?

Static electricity! When you run a plastic comb through your dry hair several times and bring it near bits of paper, they stick to the comb. When you run the comb on your hair, it gets charged and acquires a force in the form of static electricity. This pulls the bits of paper towards the comb.

Why doesn't glue stick to the bottle it is in?

Because there's no air! Glue contains water and chemicals. When you apply glue on something you want it to stick, water in the glue comes in contact with air and evaporates. This makes things stick together. But when glue is inside a bottle, the water in the glue does not get enough air to evaporate. This keeps the glue in its liquid state and doesn't get stuck on the bottle!

Pocket fact

Super Glue!
Super Glue was invented accidently by Harry Coover while attempting to make plastic lenses for rifle sights. It was impossible to work with this glue because it stuck to everything!

Find out

Who was the first person to invent cement?

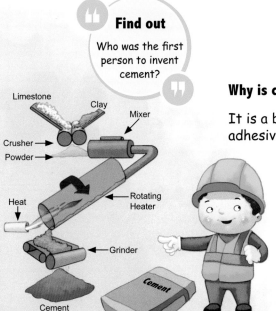

Why is cement strong enough to bind bricks?

It is a binder, like glue! Cement acts as an adhesive when it dries and holds bricks and stones together. It is made by heating clay and limestone in a big oven called a kiln. Heating brings changes in the metals, and a hard substance called clinker is made. Clinker is powdered and mixed with gypsum, a soft white or grey coloured mineral. This makes cement ready for use!

Why does a pencil look bent in a glass of water?

Because of refraction of light! Refraction is a change in direction of light when it travels through different medium. Light travels in air, vacuum and water at different speeds. When light enters water, it cannot move as fast as it does in air. On entering water, refraction occurs. Light bends away from its path. This is why the pencil (or any object) immersed in a glass of water, appears bent.

Light Waves

Find out

What is the speed of sound?

Pocket fact

A lens uses refraction to form an image of an object for many different purposes. Interestingly, a prism uses refraction to form a spectrum of colours from an incident beam of light.

Why can't I hear anything in vacuum?

Because a vacuum does not have particles that can vibrate! Sound is a wave and is created when a movement causes vibrations in its surrounding particles (atoms or molecules), usually a gas or liquid. Atoms and molecules are found everywhere except in a vacuum. When sound vibrations reach the tiny hair in your ear drum, you hear sound. Since there are no molecules in vacuum, no vibrations occur. The sound doesn't travel and you cannot hear anything.

Why is a tennis ball fuzzy?

To help the ball move at a balanced speed! A tennis ball is fuzzy because it allows the ball to move forward without increasing its speed too much. When the tennis ball strikes the racquet, it lightly grips the ball's fuzz and controls its movement. When the ball moves at slower speeds, the fuzz allows it to move faster and when the ball reaches a higher speed, the fuzz helps control the speed of the tennis ball.

Find out

Why does a golf ball have dimples?

Pocket fact

Tyres were white too!
Tyres were white for the first 25 years after the invention of cars. This was because zinc oxide was added to the rubber in order to make them strong. This gave tyres the bright white colour.

Why are tyres black?

For their protection! Vehicle tyres are black because a chemical called carbon black is mixed in them during the manufacturing process. This increases the strength of the tyres and also protects them against the harmful ultra violet (UV) rays from the sun. Sun's UV rays can wear out and crack the tyres. Carbon black converts the UV radiations into heat thus protecting the tyre.

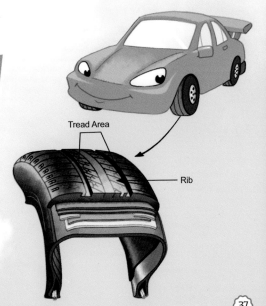

Tread Area

Rib

Why do some cooking utensils have wooden or plastic handles?

Plastic Handle

To protect you from getting burnt! Cooking utensils are made of metals that are good conductors of heat. If the handles are also made of metals, they will absorb heat. So, if you pick a utensil by the metal handle, it can burn you! On the other hand, wood and some durable plastics do not allow heat to pass through them. So handles made of wood or plastic make it easy for you to handle cooking utensils.

" Pocket fact

The most widely used material for cookware (on gas stoves) are stainless steel, copper and aluminium. Stainless steel is made by adding chromium and nickel to steel. This makes it highly anti-corrosive. "

" Find out

Who made teflon first? "

Teflon Layer

Why doesn't food stick on non-stick pans?

Because it has no friction at all! Non-stick pans have a coating of teflon layer. Teflon is known as polytetrafluoroethylene (PTFE), a compound of carbon and fluorine. The coating of teflon on non-stick pans makes the pans smooth and slippery. The smoothness of the surface offers no friction. The lack of friction doesn't allow food to get stuck on these pans.

Find out

From which plant is menthol extracted?

Why does mint gum make my mouth feel cold?

The secret is menthol! Mint gum contains menthol that binds with cold-sensitive receptors in your skin. These receptors have some channels called TRPM8. The menthol makes these receptors very sensitive and gives you a cold sensation. The sensation is colder if you drink water just after having a mint gum!

Pocket fact

Chlorine in salt!
Chlorine is found in the most common substance we use in our food. It is sodium chloride better known as 'common salt'.

Why is chlorine added to swimming pool water?

To kill bacteria! The water in a swimming pool may be infected with bacteria as a lot of people use the pool. When we go for a swim, bacteria from our bodies escape into the pool. When chlorine gas (in its liquid form) is added directly to the water, a hypochlorite ion is formed. This ion releases oxygen. The released oxygen then reacts with all organic matter and kills the bacteria!

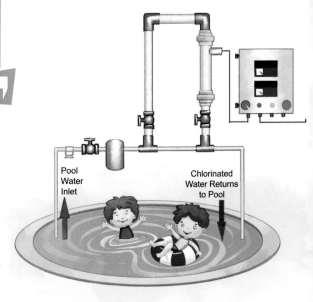

Pool Water Inlet

Chlorinated Water Returns to Pool

Why is water colourless?

Because it absorbs all the colours of white light! White light is made of seven colours. When light falls on an object, it absorbs some colours and reflects others. The reflected colour reaches our eyes and the object appears to be of that colour. For example: when you look at mango juice, all colours from the light are absorbed, except yellow. Yellow colour reaches our eyes and therefore the juice looks yellow. When light falls on water, it reflects all colours, expect a tiny tint of blue. This makes water appear transparent and colourless.

Pocket fact

Hot water freezes faster!
It is interesting to know that hot water freezes faster than cold water. This is known as the Mpemba Effect. No one knows the secret behind it!

Try this

Can you list names of any five things that do not dissolve in water?

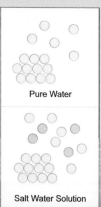

Pure Water

Salt Water Solution

Why does adding salt to water make it freeze slowly?

Salt lowers the freezing point of water! Water changes to ice at a temperature of 0 °Celsius. This temperature is called the freezing point of water. When you add salt to it, salt molecules occupy space between water molecules and the water molecules repel these salt molecules. This makes it harder for water molecules to bond the ice structure thus preventing water from freezing at 0 °Celsius.

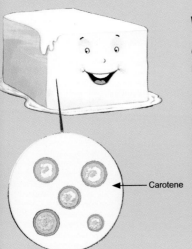

Why is butter usually yellow?

Carotene gives butter its colour! Butter has a natural pigment carotene. Carotene is fat soluble, it is transferred to milk fat and then into the butter, giving it the yellow tint. The amount of carotene depends on a cow's feed. Cows feed mostly on hay, silage, grains and cereals, which produce carotene rich dairy. Sometimes, artificial pigments are also added to butter to enhance the yellow colour. When the amount of carotene is low, butter gets a natural white colour instead of yellow.

Carotene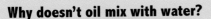

 Pocket fact

Marigold flowers to colour butter! Artificial colour has been added to butter since about 800 years! During the Middle Ages marigold flowers were used to enhance the yellow colour of the butter.

 Find out

What do you call two liquids that do not mix with each other?

Why doesn't oil mix with water?

Both behave differently with each other! Water molecules have a small positive (+) charge at one end, and a small negative (-) charge at the other end, so they stick to each other. But oil molecules don't have any charge. This is why they are not attracted to water molecules but to each other. This prevents oil from mixing with water. In fact, oil floats on water because it is less dense than water.

Why do jet planes leave a trail of smoke behind?

Water and carbon dioxide form the trail! Jet planes fly 26,000 feet above the sea level. The air is very cold at such a great height. As a jet plane flies, hot water vapour and carbon dioxide is released from its engine which come in contact with the freezing air outside. So, water vapour changes to water and ice particles immediately. These particles attract more water molecules towards them and the tiny drops of water form clouds. This leaves a trail called contrail as the jet moves forward!

Contrail

Pocket fact

Fastest jet plane!
The world's fastest manned jet airplane is the U.S. Air Force's SR-71 Blackbird. It flies at more than 3,220 kilometres per hour.

Find out

How many wheels does an aeroplane usually have?

Why do aeroplanes need wheels?

To help them take off and land! The wheels of an airplane support it when it is not in air, allowing it to take off and land without damage. Aeroplanes need to move forward to maintain lift. The wheels reduce friction with the runway. This makes airplane move more easily while taking off, while landing the friction reduces the movement helping the plane to stop smoothly.

Why do moth balls keep moths away from clothes?

By emitting vapour! Moth balls are small balls made of either naphthalene or para dichlorobenzene. The chemicals, naphthalene and dichlorobenzene undergo sublimation, i.e, they evaporate from a solid state directly into a gaseous state. This gas is toxic to moth and its larvae and thus keeps moths away from our clothes!

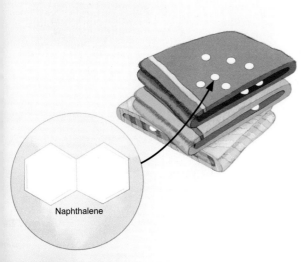

Naphthalene

Pocket fact

The first artificial sponges! Artificial sponges were first developed by the Du Pont Company in the 1940s.

Find out

What is naphthalene made from?

Why does sponge absorb so much water easily?

Loose fibres help it absorb water! A sponge is made of loose fibres that have empty space in it. This empty space gives sponge all its properties. The empty space between the fibres soak up water. This causes the fibrous material to swell and stops the water from escaping the sponge. The water is trapped inside the sponge until you squeeze it!

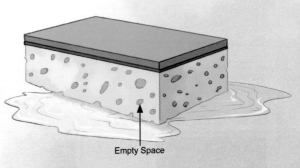

Empty Space

Why does jelly wobble?

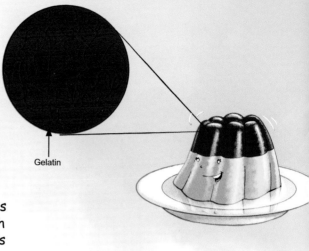

Gelatin

Because it has gelatin! Jelly is made from gelatin and fruit flavours. When gelatin molecules are warmed in water they are long, but when cooled some of these get intertwined with others and form a bigger molecule, which also branches out like a tree. This process continues and forms new 'supermolecules' and form a 'net' stretched across the material. This net makes the jelly wobble.

Find out

When was the first commercial bubble gum made?

Pocket fact

World's biggest jelly!
In 1997, the British Army's Logistics Corp helped make the world's biggest jelly at Blackpool Zoo. It was almost 1 metre tall by 7 metre wide. It took about 12 hours to set the jelly using a blast chiller.

Why is chewing gum stretchy?

Chewing gum is made from the sap of the manilkara chicle tree. The sap is called chicle and is mainly used to make chewing gums. Chewing gums have long chains of tiny particles called atoms strung together. The strings are cross-linked and tangled with each other. This links one strand with another at several places and makes the chewing gum rubbery and stretchy.

I am made from a tree.

GUM

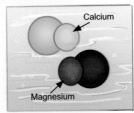

Calcium

Magnesium

Why does soap not make lather sometimes?

This happens only when hard water is used! Soap has natural fatty oils and chemicals like sodium hydroxide. When you use soap in water, a frothy white mass of bubbles is produced by it. This is called lather. Soap doesn't form lather when used in hard water. Hard water contains a lot of calcium and magnesium salts. These salts cause the soap to precipitate and it can't form lather.

SOAP

Pocket fact

Soap for elephants!
Besides human, soaps are used for cleaning animals as well. Murphy's Oil Soap is a soap used especially to clean elephants!

Find out

Who discovered chlorine as a bleaching agent?

BLEACH

Why does bleach make clothes white?

It releases oxygen! Chemical compounds called chromophores reflect a certain part of the visible spectrum of light and we see different colours. When bleach is applied on clothes, oxygen molecules are released in a process called oxidation. These oxygen molecules break up the chemical bonds of chromophores. The chromophores then reflect no colour thus making the clothes appear white.

Why do jumping beans jump?

They have tiny larva inside! Jumping beans are not beans but seed pods of a shrub that grows in Northern Mexico and Southwest America. These seed pods have the larva of a small grey moth inside them. The larva enters the seed pod and eats it, once the seed is eaten, the larva lives inside the empty pod. When you warm these beans the larva start wiggling and makes the beans jump!

Larva

Find out

Name the shrub on which jumping beans grow.

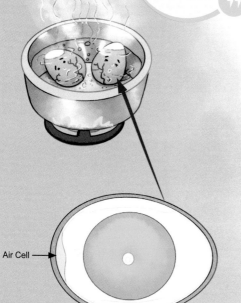

Air Cell

Pocket fact

Raw or hard boiled?
You can tell if an egg is raw or hard-boiled by simply spinning it! A hard boiled egg spins easily but a raw egg wobbles.

Why do some eggs crack while boiling?

Because they have air inside! The bottom, rounded end of an egg has a small air bubble. When you boil an egg, it heats up and the air inside the bubble expands. The hot air now pushes outwards and puts pressure onto the shell. This makes the shell crack, as a result some eggs crack while boiling.

Copper Wire

Plastic Coating

Why are electric wires covered with plastic?

To prevent us from getting an electric shock! Electric wires are made of copper that is a good conductor of electricity. But these wires are coated with rubber or plastic because both plastic and rubber are bad conductors of electricity. So, when you touch the wire, you won't get an electric shock since plastic doesn't allow electricity to reach your body. Also, plastic is flexible and bends easily around corners and fits into electrical boxes safely.

Find out

Why do wires in electric appliances or switches have different colours?

Why do most ceiling fans have three blades?

To push more air as it rotates! A ceiling fan circulates air, making us feel cool. The air circulates when the blades of the fan cut the path of air with its blades and pushes the air downwards. The air pushed by the fan depends on the number of blades it has. If there are more blades, the volume of the air to push is less but speed of air is high. If the number of blades is less the volume of air is more but the speed of air is slower. Since a fan cannot have just one blade, the balance is usually maintained by having 2 or 3 blades.

Pocket fact

First ceiling fan!
The inventor of the ceiling fan developed the electric motor used in the electrically-powered sewing machines. He then used that motor to use in a ceiling-mounted fan.

Blades

When?

HELLo

ECHO
POINT

When does an iron nail behave like a magnet?

When electricity is passed through it! If you wrap an iron nail in coils of electric wire and pass electricity through it, the nail behaves like a powerful magnet. Such a magnet is called a solenoid. The nail loses its magnetic property when you switch off the electricity supply.

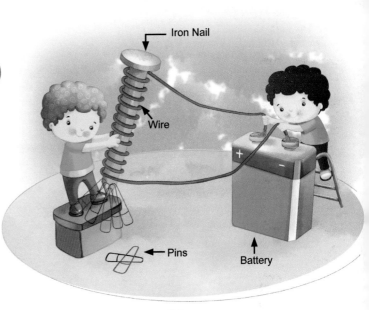

Iron Nail

Wire

Pins

Battery

Pocket fact

The Liberty Bell in Pennsylvania, USA, is made of the alloy bronze. This bell is an iconic symbol of American independence.

Find out

Name an electric appliance that uses electromagnets.

When can I call a metal an alloy?

When a metal is mixed with another metal! Sometimes metals are mixed with other metals or substances to create new materials. These materials are called alloys. For instance, copper and tin are mixed to form an alloy called bronze. Similarly, copper and zinc are used to make brass. Alloys are created to make materials stronger and they also help retain a metal's shine.

Bronze Statue

When was the first completely human-made plastic invented?

In 1905! Belgian chemist, Leo Baekeland, created the first human-made plastic. He used the chemicals phenol and formaldehyde to make this plastic. It was named Bakelite. Bakelite was used to manufacture many things, such as telephone handsets, costume jewellery, bases and sockets for light bulbs, automobile engine parts and washing machine components.

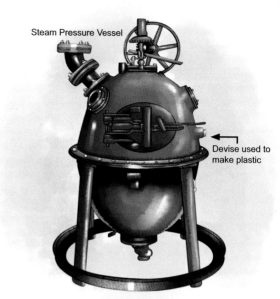

Steam Pressure Vessel

← Devise used to make plastic

Find out

Which plant gives us the guar gum needed to make slime?

Pocket fact

The word plastic comes from the Greek word 'plasticos'. It means to be shaped or moulded by heat.

4% Solution PVA

Distilled Water

Store ⇒

← Borax

4 gm of Borax in 100 ml of distilled water

Store ⇒

Heat

Ratio: 5 parts PVA 1 part borax

Colouring →

← Slime

When was slime first made?

In 1976! Just as its name suggests, slime is an unpleasant, thick and slippery substance. It is a play material that was manufactured in 1976 by a toy manufacturing company. It consists of a non-toxic, viscous, oozing green material. The main chemicals used to make slime are the polysaccharide guar gum and sodium tetraborate.

When was electricity first stored in a jar?

Between 1745 and 1746! A German cleric, Ewald Georg Von Kleist, and a Dutch scientist, Pieter Van Musschenbroek invented a jar that stored static electricity between two electrodes on the inner and outer surfaces of a glass jar. This jar was known as the Leyden jar. It had a glass jar with metal foil fixed on the inner and outer surfaces, and a metal terminal going up through the jar lid so that it could be connected with the inner foil and store electricity.

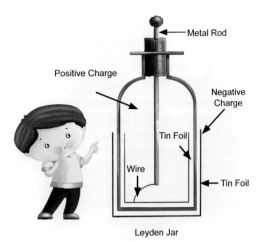

Metal Rod

Positive Charge

Negative Charge

Tin Foil

Wire

Tin Foil

Leyden Jar

Try this
Dancing balloons
- Blow up 2 balloons.
- Tie a string onto the end of each balloon.
- Give each balloon a static charge by rubbing it with fur, wool, or your hair.
- Now hold each balloon by the end of the string and bring the balloons close to each other.
  What happens? Did the balloons dance?

Pocket fact
World's largest battery!
The world's largest battery is in Fairbanks, Alaska, USA. It is a type of rechargeable battery that has nickel oxide hydroxide and metallic cadmium.

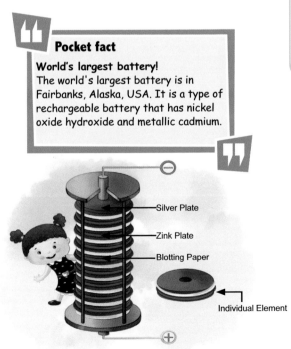

Silver Plate

Zink Plate

Blotting Paper

Individual Element

When was the first battery made to create electricity?

In 1800! Alessandro Volta developed the voltaic pile, the first battery that created electricity from chemicals. It consisted of pairs of copper and zinc discs piled on top of each other. These were separated by a layer of cloth or cardboard soaked in brine. The voltaic pile produced a continuous and stable current, but also lost little charge when not in use.

When does water begin to boil?

When it reaches 100 °Celsius! Boiling is the process by which liquids begin to change from their liquid state to the gaseous state. Water starts boiling at 100 °Celsius. However, this temperature is not fixed. Water boils at a lower temperature in high altitude areas. Besides this, if water contains impurities (such as salts), it boils at a higher temperature.

Water

Find out

What is the process that turns liquid into vapour?

Pocket fact

A gypsum desert!
A large gypsum desert is located in New Mexico. It is known as White Sands National Monument and is operated by the US National Park Service. The gypsum desert is over 710 square kilometres in size.

When does gypsum release water?

When it is heated! Gypsum is a soft rock that can be scratched easily. It has a unique property of releasing water when it is exposed to heat. This makes gypsum useful in making drywalls for homes and buildings. It burns easily, like wood, but, at the same time, has the added fire protection benefit of releasing some water.

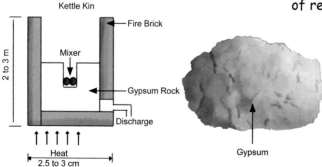

Kettle Kin

Fire Brick

Mixer

2 to 3 m

Gypsum Rock

Discharge

Heat
2.5 to 3 cm

Gypsum

Asphalt Cement

When does asphalt cement show plastic behaviour?

When it is heated to 60°Celsius! Asphalt cement is a highly viscous material. A viscous material is one that can flow. Asphalt cement behaves like a viscous liquid and flows when it is heated to 60°Celsius! or more. This is called plastic behaviour because after the asphalt cement has flowed, it does not return to its original position.

Pocket fact

The word diamond comes from the Greek word 'adamas', which means invincible or indestructible. Diamonds are, in fact, the hardest natural substance. True to its name, the only thing that can scratch or cut a diamond is another diamond.

Find out

List one use of asphalt cement.

When was the largest diamond found?

In 1905! The largest diamond was discovered at the Premier Mine in South Africa on January 25, 1905. It was a 3,106-carat diamond, weighing 603.2779 grams. The diamond was found during a routine inspection by the mine's superintendent, Sir Thomas Cullinan and is named 'Cullinan' after him.

When applied pressure! Quartz is a mineral that is widely found in igneous and metamorphic rocks, such as granite, rhyolite, schist, gneiss, etc. Quartz is formed in the form of hexagonal prisms. Quartz crystals have piezoelectric properties; they develop an electric charge when pressure is applied. For this reason, quartz is used in mechanical watches and when pressure is applied by the DC motor of the watch, quartz makes the hands of the watch move.

Quartz

Hexagonal Prisms

Find out

Which mineral does limestone consist?

Pocket fact

Different shades!
Quartz can be found in various colours like, purple, red, black, yellow, brown, blue, colourless, green, rose, orange, etc. All the forms of quartz are displayed in the Smithsonian Museum of Natural History, USA.

Limestone

Marble

Prototlith

5x Limestone
(Sedimentary Rock)

Non-Foliated Metamorphic rock

5x Marble

When does limestone change into marble?

When limestone is exposed to high temperature and pressure! Marble is a rock. It is formed from limestone when it is affected by heat and high pressure during a process known as metamorphosis. During metamorphosis, the structure of limestone's crystals changes, which in turn changes it into a denser rock. This denser rock is called marble.

Iron Oxide

When do objects rust?

Some objects rust when they are exposed to moisture and air! Rust is a reddish brown compound called iron oxide. Only objects that are made of iron and steel can rust. When iron objects are exposed to air and water, iron reacts with oxygen in the air and forms a compound called iron oxide, or rust, and this corrodes iron.

Find out

Which metal is used in thermometers?

When do metals expand?

On heating! Metals usually expand upon heating. All substances are made of tiny particles called molecules and so are metals. When a metal is heated, its molecules start vibrating about and tend to move further apart. This makes them expand.

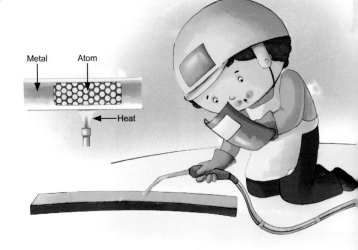

Metal   Atom

Heat

When does a flame turn blue?

When it gets more oxygen! A flame is usually yellow in colour. But, the colour of a flame can be orange and blue too. A flame's colour is determined by certain factors, such as the substance that emits the flame and the oxygen available to it. A flame is yellow because of the incandescence of the fine soot particles (flaky substance containing carbon) that glow. When oxygen increases, there is less soot and the flame burns blue.

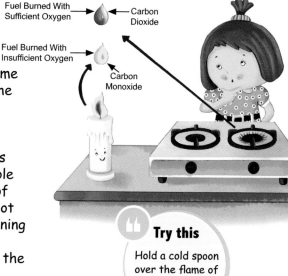

Fuel Burned With Sufficient Oxygen — Carbon Dioxide

Fuel Burned With Insufficient Oxygen — Carbon Monoxide

Try this

Hold a cold spoon over the flame of a candle. What happens?

Pocket fact

Spirits of camphor!
Camphor is insoluble in water but soluble in alcohol, ether, chloroform and other solvents. When camphor is dissolved in alcohol, the alcoholic solution formed is known as spirits of camphor.

When does camphor turn to a liquid?

Never! A camphor changes directly to vapour when it is heated. All substances are made of particles called molecules which are held together by forces between them. The particles of some substances have strong forces but some have weak. The molecules of camphor are held together by very weak forces. So, when you heat camphor it simply evaporates and changes to vapour without changing to a liquid first.

When does sugar caramelise?

On heating! Caramelisation is a reaction by which sugar turns brown when it is heated to a certain temperature. Besides giving sugar a brown colour, this process gives it a nutty flavour. It is a widely used method in cooking. The caramelisation of sugar depends on the type of sugar. Sucrose and glucose caramelise at around 160 °Celsius and fructose caramelises at 110 °Celsius.

Sugar Being Heated

Caramelised Sugar

Pocket fact

National Caramel Day!
Caramel is a beloved treat in the United States. The people of US celebrate National Caramel Day on April 5th every year!

Find out

What is the meaning of the word 'vinegar'?

When does vinegar freeze?

Vinegar is made up of water and a chemical known as acetic acid. On its own, acetic acid usually freezes at 16.6 °Celsius. However, because vinegar has water and acetic acid, the freezing point of the acid drops below 0 °Celsius. The temperature at which vinegar freezes depends on the amount of acetic acid present in it. The more acetic acid vinegar has, the quicker it will freeze. Common commercially-produced vinegar contains five percent acetic acid and freezes at approximately -2 °Celsius.

Plain water freezes at 4 °Celsius

Apple cider vinegar freezes at -2 °Celsius

When does a sound become an echo?

When sound waves reflect back! Echoes are commonly heard when loud sounds are emitted into an empty room, down a well or on high mountains. When you make a sound, most of it is absorbed by objects around. But at some places, such as empty rooms or wells, sound waves reflect back to the source after hitting a hard surface (like the walls of the room or well). This reflected sound is called an echo.

Pocket fact

Let's sing!
Whales can communicate with each other by making sounds. This is called 'singing' to each other. Their song can travel a distance of 800 kilometres!

Find out

What is the fear of thunder and lightning called?

When does a thunder occur?

When particles in a cloud vibrate and collide! Thunder is the sound that is heard during a thunderstorm and this is usually accompanied by lightning. You can hear sound due to vibrations in particles of a gas or liquid. The vibrations travel as a sound wave through the air, until they reach your ear. During a thunderstorm a lightning bolt travels from the cloud to the ground. The air in the cloud collapses in, make the particles vibrate and collide. This creates a sound wave called thunder!

When can a fire burn underwater?

In an underwater torch! Water is used to put out fire, but an underwater torch keeps the flame alive! An underwater torch works by providing a source of oxygen and hydrogen or acetylene that burns to produce a flame. It has two hoses. When the hoses are activated, hydrogen (or acetylene) combines with the oxygen and produces a flame at the tip of the torch. To keep the flame alive underwater, hydrogen must be exerted at a high pressure. Underwater torches have a number of spouts that emit compressed air around the tip of the torch. This air lessens the pressure of the water and keeps the flame lit.

Find out

Which metal can burn when exposed to air or water?

Underwater Torch

Pocket fact

A famous superior mirage is the Fata Morgana. It is most frequently seen in the Strait of Messina between Italy and Sicily.

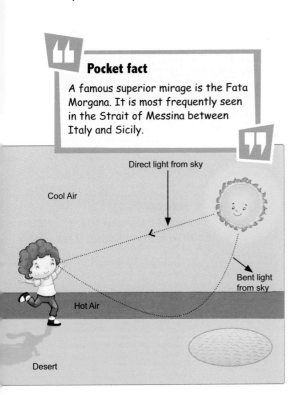

Direct light from sky

Cool Air

Bent light from sky

Hot Air

Desert

When does a mirage occur?

When light bends through air at different temperatures! A mirage is an illusion of water on hot lands. Light travels at different speeds through different mediums, even through hot air and cold air. Mirages occur when the ground is very hot and the air is cool. The hot ground warms a layer of air just above it. When sunlight moves from the layer of cold air to the layer of hot air, it bends and forms a U-shape reflection. This seems like a puddle of water to us.

When can a bulb fuse?

When it gets more electric current than needed! A bulb needs a specific amount of electricity to glow. All bulbs have a fuse plugged into them. This fuse contains a piece of a special wire that melts easily. When a bulb gets more electric current than required, the fuse wire heats up and melts. This stops the flow of current and thus you say that the bulb has 'fused'.

Find out

Who invented the electric fuse?

Pocket fact

Too fast!
Electrical current is a measure of the speed at which particles called electrons flow through a circuit. The speed at which electrons flow is often close to the speed of light which is 1,079,252,850 kilometres per hour!

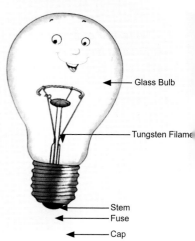

Glass Bulb

Tungsten Filament

Stem
Fuse
Cap

When does an electric short circuit occur?

When there is an excessive supply of current! A short circuit is a connection between two conductors of an electric circuit that supply electrical power to it. A short circuit occurs when the positive and negative terminals of a battery are connected with a conductor that allows easy flow of electricity without controlling it. When there is a high flow of electricity, the conductors deliver a large amount of energy in a short time and can also cause the wires to explode!

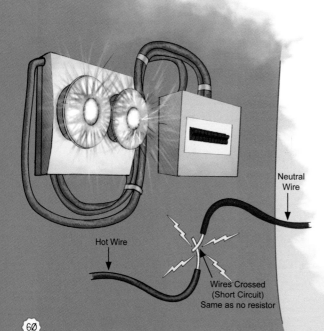

Neutral Wire

Hot Wire

Wires Crossed
(Short Circuit)
Same as no resistor

When was paper made?

Around 3000 years ago! Nowadays, paper is made from the wood of fast-growing trees such as fir, pine and spruce. But the Chinese were to invent it first! Paper was invented in China around 100 BC, a Chinese official named Ts'ai Lun made his paper by mixing finely chopped mulberry bark and hemp rags with water. He mashed the mixture, then pressed out water and let it dry in the sunlight.

Find out

Is nylon waterproof?

Pocket fact

First paper merchant!
Benjamin Franklin was the first paper merchant in USA. He helped start 18 paper mills in Virginia and its surrounding areas. Cotton and linen rags were the papermaker's raw materials at that time.

Nylon 6

Nylon 6,6

When was nylon invented?

In 1935! Nylon is a thermoplastic silky material widely used in toothbrush bristles, socks, fishing nets, carpets and many other items. Nylon was first produced on February 28, 1935, by Wallace Carothers. Nylon is made of repeated chains of molecules called polymers!

Index

OTHER TITLES IN THIS SERIES

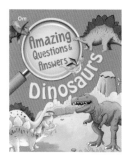

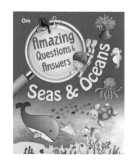